HOW TO HELP AN ADDICT

*Pulling the Addict Out of
Hopelessness and into Freedom*

Paul Simmerman

How to Help an Addict
Pulling the Addict Out of Hopelessness and into Freedom
Copyright © 2019 by Paul Simmerman

Scripture quotations marked TPT are from The Passion Translation®. Copyright © 2017, 2018 by Passion & Fire Ministries, Inc. Used by permission. All rights reserved. ThePassionTranslation.com
Scripture quotations marked NASB are from the New American Standard Bible®,
Copyright © 1960, 1962, 1963, 1968, 1971, 1972, 1973,
1975, 1977, 1995 by The Lockman Foundation
Used by permission. www.Lockman.org

Printed in the United States of America

First Printing: Jan 2019

ISBN - 9781793391636

"For now we see but a faint reflection of riddles and mysteries as though reflected in a mirror, but one day we will see face-to-face. My understanding is incomplete now, but one day I will understand everything, just as everything about me has been fully understood. [13] Until then, there are three things that remain: faith, hope, and love—yet love surpasses them all. So above all else, let love be the beautiful prize for which you run."

—1 CORINTHIANS 13: 12–13, TPT

I dedicate this book to the ultimate Redeemer, my Lord Jesus Christ. Without God's love, compassion, patience, forgiveness and redemption, I would still be wandering in the wilderness maturing in everything that is rooted in lies and my destruction. It is, under no uncertain terms, God who delivered me and keeps me. My life is His.

ACKNOWLEDGEMENTS

THERE ARE SO MANY PEOPLE that have contributed to my wellness over the past 14 years of sobriety. My brother opened his home to me in the first year and my dad invested in me all my life. I always say that it took my mom returning to Heaven sooner than any of us wanted to get me there with her. I'm convinced that she turned up the heat on God once she was face to face with Him. I have this vision of her really insisting on Him delivering me from addiction. I know she was a prayer warrior in this while here on earth. My aunts, uncles and cousins were also very patient and supportive of me. The AA program and its' members were instrumental in my sobriety. Especially Geoff, Paul, and Kenny. That could be the understatement of the century. My wife Stacey who has made it possible for me to live a life that I could only dream about. My children, Audrey and Paul, who teach me way more than I teach them. My father in-law/Pastor, Spike, who encouraged me to write this book. I thank you all for helping me by loving me.

CONTENTS

Acknowledgements 5

Introduction From my Wife..7

Part One: Understanding the Addict 9

Understanding the Addict 10

Believing Lies..13

The Spirit of Suicide 15

The Spirits of Guilt and Shame...17

The Spirit of Victim 19

Judgement...21

Part Two: Hope, Repentance, Deliverance.................................22

What Really Happened 23

Faith..25

Hope..27

Love 31

Part Three: The Power of Testimony...33

Testimony 34

Conclusion..36

INTRODUCTION FROM
MY WIFE

THIS BOOK IS A GOLD MINE! If you have an addict in your life, and most of us do, you know how difficult it is to watch them go through life in bondage. It is frustrating, fearful, and even enraging at times.

I met Paul when he was 3 years sober, so I never knew him before he was delivered from addiction. There have been so many times people from his past would see him with me and our kids in the grocery store or somewhere, and a look of pure shock would be plastered to their face. I am not sure if they were surprised he was still alive, or in disbelief that he had a family or what. I would comment about this to Paul after the encounter and he would just smile and say, "I don't really know how to even explain to you how bad off I was. You had to see it to believe it I guess." I tell you this because a lot of times we tend to feel like the addict we know is beyond help. That they will never change. Believe me when I tell you, Paul is proof that even those deepest in bondage can be pulled out.

Many people ask Paul to help them with their loved ones. I hear them say, "can you talk to them?" And Paul is always willing, if the person is agreeable. It seems to me however, after reading what Paul has written in this book, that the best people to have an impact on the addict are those who know and love them the best- and that's YOU! You just need some tools to do so. You just need to understand a little better what is really going on with them. You need to get a vision of God's thoughts about the situation. This book will help you do that.

I am so grateful that God delivered Paul from addiction and put him in our lives. God wants the same for your loved one, and it CAN happen.

PART ONE: UNDERSTANDING THE ADDICT

UNDERSTANDING THE ADDICT

TO EFFECTIVELY HELP AN ADDICT, it's important to understand the addict. The addict is living in a seemingly open prison cell. I lived imprisoned by addiction for twenty years (13 to 33 years old). The entire twenty years, I knew it was wrong and that I needed to stop. I knew it was killing me and separating me from everything I ever cared for or about. I saw that "drinkers" didn't even want to be around me, let alone "non-drinkers". I could feel the destruction to my body, soul, and spirit. By far the best description of how I felt inside is found in Romans 7:9-24.

"9-10 I once lived without a clear understanding of the law, but when I heard God's commandments, sin sprang to life and brought with it a death sentence. The commandment that was intended to bring life brought me death instead. 11 Sin, by means of the commandment, built a base of operation within me, to overpower me and put me to death. 12 So then, we have to conclude that the problem is not with the law itself, for the law is holy and its commandments are correct and for our good.

13 So, did something meant to be good become death to me? Certainly not! It was not the law but sin unmasked that produced my spiritual death. The sacred commandment merely uncovered the evil of sin so it could be seen for what it is. 14 For we know that the law is divinely inspired and comes from the spiritual realm, but I am a human being made of flesh and trafficked as a slave under sin's authority.

15 I'm a mystery to myself, for I want to do what is right, but end up doing what my moral instincts condemn. 16 And if my behavior is not in

line with my desire, my conscience still confirms the excellence of the law. [17] And now I realize that it is no longer my true self doing it, but the unwelcome intruder of sin in my humanity. [18] For I know that nothing good lives within the flesh of my fallen humanity. The longings to do what is right are within me, but will-power is not enough to accomplish it. [19] My lofty desires to do what is good are dashed when I do the things I want to avoid. [20] So if my behavior contradicts my desires to do good, I must conclude that it's not my true identity doing it, but the unwelcome intruder of sin hindering me from being who I really am.

[21] Through my experience of this principle, I discover that even when I want to do good, evil is ready to sabotage me. [22] Truly, deep within my true identity, I love to do what pleases God. [23] But I discern another power operating in my humanity, waging a war against the moral principles of my conscience and bringing me into captivity as a prisoner to the "law" of sin—this unwelcome intruder in my humanity. [24] What an agonizing situation I am in! So who has the power to rescue this miserable man from the unwelcome intruder of sin and death? [25] I give all my thanks to God, for his mighty power has finally provided a way out through our Lord Jesus, the Anointed One! So if left to myself, the flesh is aligned with the law of sin, but now my renewed mind is fixed on and submitted to God's righteous principles" (Romans 7:9-24 The Passion Translation).

When people attempted to help me by telling me that I needed to stop, it worked in the opposite way. That instruction or command just reinforced that I was a failure. When people told me that I needed to stop drinking/drugging, it verified or reinforced the lie that I was a hopeless failure. Addiction is fueled by hopelessness. Hopelessness is the unwanted spirit that verifies the lies that addicts believe. I know it's hard to relate to this idea, but it's necessary to understand it.

I tried to stop drinking several times. My attempts were terribly misguided, but never the less, I wanted to stop. I can remember telling a couple of friends that I needed to stop drinking for a while. "I need to take a break." The wife of this couple worked across the street from me and the husband would pick us both up from work. I had lost my driving privileges at the time. I remember one night, only 2 or 3 days into my much needed break, I finished work first and I had to kill some time. I ended up at the nearby bar drinking like "normal". When the couple found me, which wasn't hard to do, the wife said to me, "I thought you were taking a break?" I'll never forget the way I felt at that moment. The feeling of hopelessness and imprisonment. I wanted to stop drinking so bad, but here I was, failing yet again. My identity had been stolen in such a way that I could only see myself and refer to myself as an alcoholic and drug addict. This was one of many illustrations of how my true nature and identity wanted out of the lie that had me imprisoned. As Holy Spirt teaches me about my future through my testimony, I can see how my true identity was literally trying to fight its way out of the false costume that the lies were causing me to wear.

BELIEVING LIES

IN MY IMPRISONMENT, I BELIEVED LIES about myself that have nothing to do with the Truth of how and who I was truly created to be. I believed I was a terrible person. That word has nothing to do with God. God is not terrible and He doesn't create terrible things. Hence it being a lie. When people would say to me, "You look terrible", it reinforced the lie that I believed about myself. I know that those people weren't intentionally trying to do this, or maybe some were, who knows. I know that my loved ones and relatives were not trying to hurt me. They were coming from a place of not relating to or understanding what was happening to me. They were responding or reacting to what they were seeing in the natural. Their response or reaction was being shaped by life's circumstances. My life circumstances were making me look terrible. Again, the costume that I was wearing. I can recall the pain and desperation in their faces, as they were trying to do whatever they could to help me. At least what they thought could help me. Please understand that I don't, in any way, blame or hold this against anyone that said these things to me. I know that those who love me are good hearted people with good intentions. They were NOT the cause of my addiction. I never believed for a minute that they consciously or deliberately contributed to my imprisonment. They were doing the best they could with what they were equipped with.

The most common thought pattern in trying to help an addict is, "I'm going to snap them out of it." This thought pattern needs to be changed to, "I'm going to PULL them out of it." Pointing out how awful the person is keeps them imprisoned in the lies they are believing. **Pulling the addict out of their costume of lies by speaking to the person that God created**

them to be is really the only way to help them. Believe me when I say that the person God created them to be is dying to be freed from the lies. Literally and figuratively.

THE SPIRIT OF SUICIDE

THE UNWANTED SPIRITS THAT AFFLICTED ME the most during my twenty years of addiction were hopelessness, suicide, guilt, shame, and victim. It was these spirits, or demons if you will, that lied to me. That's what they do, they lie. They are followers of the father of lies.

My imprisonment was also a long term suicide attempt. I don't think people realize how much these unwanted spirits, demons, work together to devour God's children. The spirit of suicide is one of the prison guards. I know you have heard an addict say, "I'm only hurting myself". This comes from the spirit of suicide. My drinking and drugging became a self-inflicted punishment. Because I thought so poorly of myself, I believed the lie that I deserved to be punished. Along with that, I believed that I DID NOT deserve forgiveness, grace, or mercy. This lie is the root of the destructiveness and self-inflicted punishment. I know what I'm about to tell you seems insane. That's because it is insane.

The very last time I drank was arguably the most intoxicated I had ever been in my life. I had no idea, or intention, that it was going to be the last time I drank, but that's how it ended up. I had gotten in trouble yet again and I was being forced into the rooms of AA in order to keep my driver's license. I was planning to attend my first of 3 meetings that I was required to attend, on a Sunday morning. The unwanted spirits in my life must have known what God was going to do, because they took their best shot at destroying me the night before that meeting. I literally had the thought, "I'll make those AAers suffer for making me go to this." So I proceeded to pour a nearly lethal amount of alcohol, along with drugs, into myself.

There are two things that are crazy insane about this, but it will explain the lie that I was believing. First, I was trying to make the people in AA suffer. They weren't the people that forced me into the rooms. The legal system forced me. More than that, I forced myself. My breaking the law and driving drunk forced me. The second thing and most absurd, was that by nearly killing myself I was going to make someone else suffer.

This is what the spirit of suicide does. It caused me to want to punish myself in ways, for reasons, that didn't make any rational sense. Regularly, for about three years prior to my deliverance, I can remember waking up in the morning in disbelief that I survived the day and night before. I didn't consciously make an attempt on my own life, but I didn't care if I lived or died. I had zero regard or value for my life, because I believed the lie that the spirit of suicide was telling me. I believed that I deserved to die. So when people would say to me, "You're killing yourself" or "You're hurting yourself", it verified the lie that I was believing. In my brokenness, I heard "See, you're right, you do deserve to die," when people were really just trying to get me to see what I was doing. I could see what I was doing, but I was coming from a place of brokenness and lies, so it sounded different than it was intended.

THE SPIRITS OF GUILT AND SHAME

I PUT THE SPIRITS OF GUILT AND SHAME together because they work so closely with each other. Guilt and Shame cause pain. Guilt is the blame I put on myself, "It's my fault." Shame is the condemnation, "I'm a bad person because I did that." Together, they literally make our hearts hurt. Addicts drink and do drugs to deal with pain. This one is particularly hard to deal with, because it has everything to do with perception.

I can remember seeing my mother's hurting face when she looked at me. She was hurting. It hurt her deeply to watch her son suffer. She didn't intend to cause me shame or guilt, but the lies I believed altered my perception to the point that even her facial expressions reinforced the lie that I was believing. Please don't get frustrated with this part of the story. I will give you solutions later in the chapters to come. I'm only trying to help you understand who and what you are dealing with when dealing with the imprisoned. Saying things like, "You're hurting me and your family members" really drives home the lie. Even if the prisoner says, "I'm only hurting myself," we know that we're hurting people around us. We know that when we ruin a holiday celebration that it hurts our loved ones. We know that when we steal, lie, cheat, or anything else that's harmful to people or ourselves that it hurts our loved ones.

The unwanted spirits of Guilt and Shame lie to us by convincing us that that's who we are and it's what we do. These demons go after our identity. Adam and Eve experienced shame and blame once they sinned (Genesis 3:8-12). Up to the point of their deception, they were unashamed (Genesis

2:25). Guilt and Shame use our sin to accuse us of being unworthy of God's love. They cause the prisoner to lose sight of the fact that they are righteous in God's sight and that through the blood of Jesus they are reconciled to God. Like Adam and Eve, I hid myself from God in shame. This is by far the worst thing that can happen to anyone. Hiding from the solution to our problem. Hiding from the Victor of every battle. God asked Adam and Eve, "Who told you that you were naked?" (Genesis 3:11a) Guilt and Shame's lies cause the addict to blame themselves and hide from God.

THE SPIRIT OF VICTIM

THE SPIRIT OF VICTIM IS AN interesting one. Though it seems to conflict with most of these other unwanted spirits that lie to us, it contributes to our stolen identity. This lie causes us to blame others ... "I'm in this situation because..." This is important to know for your own protection. The more you side with, reinforce, or confirm the lies, the more the prisoner will judge and blame you. While imprisoned, I had little to no accountability or responsibility for myself. My mindset was, and perhaps it was a defense mechanism, that it was someone else's fault that I was in the situation I was in. Even Adam blamed Eve and ultimately God for his sin.

The lie had convinced me that there were legitimate reasons to drink and to do drugs. It got so bad that the sun coming up was reason enough. I can remember going to my friend's house to watch my favorite team play football with plenty of poison. I remember saying, "I hope these are beers of celebration, instead of beers of sorrow." Either way there was going to be excessive drinking and drug use. The spirit of victim lies to the prisoner and convinces them that they "deserve" or "have a good reason" to participate in their demise. Here's another story with that insane thinking. My best friend died at 32 years old. He died because cirrhosis of the liver killed him. How did I react to his death? How did I deal with my pain? I drank and did drugs more excessively than I "normally" did. By believing that I was a victim of unfair life circumstances, I increased my intake of the exact thing that caused the unfair circumstance. I know this is hard to understand and hard to believe, but I think if you can understand the afflicted person you are trying to help, you will be more effective in helping them.

Though I believed these lies and lived in accordance to them for 20 years, I didn't start out this way. Like anything in life, there is a maturation process. This is important to understand as well. **They say that drugs and alcohol stunt your growth. The truth is that addiction redirects your maturation.** I continued to mature and grow, but I didn't mature in truth, integrity, accountability, responsibility, and most of all spiritually or relationship with God. I grew and matured in lies, guilt, shame, blame, self-loathing, separation (especially from God), and everything that is harmful to myself and others.

It's important to understand that addicts are coming from a place of lies and distorted perception. It's not that addicts are the only people that believe lies, but they are most likely to grow and mature in those lies. Hopelessness, suicide or punishment, guilt, shame, and the spirit of victim are, in my personal experience and my experience with others, the lies that fuel, support, and partner with the demonic spirit of addiction.

JUDGEMENT

ALL OF THESE LIES PARTNER with judgement. Believing lies about myself, not only caused my identity to be stolen and my perception to be distorted, it caused me to judge myself and others. The lies altered my belief structure so much that I judged myself worthy of condemnation. Once I sentenced myself to death, it was easy to judge others and receive their judgement of me. During my imprisonment, the last place in the world I wanted to be was church. Church taught me that if I sinned, which I knew I was, I was going to burn in Hell. I was taught, indirectly and sometimes directly, that God was mad at me and wanted nothing to do with me, because I was such a sinner. Self-condemnation made me extremely sensitive to judgement. Don't forget that I'm openly admitting that my perception was twisted due to believing the lies of guilt and shame. Though I believe that judgement contributes to the crippling of the church, I'm sure it was WAY weightier to me. Feeling judged, created a life-size chip on my shoulder. Despite the fact that I mostly hated myself, I was quick to defend myself from people by judging them back. I remember thinking, "I'm a drunk, but look at you" and "I do drugs, but you..."

I'm going to trust that so far I have not offended you, but instead I've offered you a very small glimpse into the internal condition of the addict. Now we can move forward into the solution.

PART TWO:
HOPE, REPENTANCE, DELIVERANCE

WHAT REALLY HAPPENED

S O WHAT HAPPENED THAT Sunday? It took eight years for Holy Spirit to show me what happened that day (Sunday, April 25, 2004), and I'll never forget it. I am, however, convinced that it's nearly a bullet proof way to help your imprisoned loved one. That morning, in my drunken haze, Holy Ghost allowed my true self, who was trapped in this costume that the lies had created, see similarities in the people sitting in the room. I can remember thinking, "These people are like me and they're staying sober." Being able to see similar people sober gave me hope. A glimmer of hope is all it took. That hope turned to repentance. Not the shameful kind that causes guilt and remorse, but the kind from Heaven that allowed me to return to God's truth and His original thoughts about me. The kind of repentance that allowed me to turn so far away from my sin that I saw Jesus. Not literally, I didn't even know what that meant at the time. My thought at the time was, "This is how I'm going to stay sober". That thought, that repentance, led me into deliverance. I literally felt the unwanted spirit of addiction leave my body. Don't stop reading just yet. I know it sounds hokey and weird, but this story is vital to the possibility of helping another person. I literally felt the alcohol and drugs drain out of my body. It felt like water draining out of a tub. Within seconds, or a minute, I was as sober as I am right now over 14 years later. Remember that I was nearly dead of alcohol poisoning just hours before this happened.

I'm sharing this part of my testimony, because this is what it takes to break out of the bondage of this imprisonment. **Hope is the key. Hope is**

the life line that pulls a person out of the custom, jail cell, of lies. Think of it this way, if you tell a prisoner that he'll never have a chance at parole or that he'll never get out of prison, how do you think he'll behave? Chances are that prisoner will never want to or try to rehabilitate. He'll accept his fate as a forever prisoner and act in accordance to that identity. He will be a prisoner until his death. Whereas if you told that same prisoner that he would be eligible for parole in a certain amount of time and with a certain amount of rehabilitation, if you gave him hope, there's a much better chance that he'll at least try to change. "Hope deferred makes the heart sick, But *when* the desire comes, *it is* a tree of life" (Proverbs 13:12, NKJV). This is a real thing. Addiction is referred to as a disease so insurance will cover rehab treatment, however there is an element to it that causes the individual's heart to literally be sick. Addiction isn't a disease, it's an unwanted spirit. Hopelessness is the illness and addiction lives on hopelessness. By instilling hope in your loved one, you heal their heart and they have the capacity and strength to let God in to repair it fully.

FAITH

*"For now we see but a faint reflection of riddles and
mysteries as though reflected in a mirror, but one day we will
see face-to-face. My understanding is incomplete now, but
one day I will understand everything, just as everything about
me has been fully understood. ¹³ Until then, there are three
things that remain: **faith**, hope, and love—yet love surpasses
them all. So above all else, let love be the beautiful prize for
which you run."*
— *1 Corinthians 13:12-13, TPT*

THE WORD FAITH IS INTERCHANGEABLE with the word belief. The root
word from which we get 'faith', the noun, is PISTIS, and 'believe', the verb,
is PISTUEO. PISTIS means faith, belief, firm persuasion, assurance, firm
conviction, faithfulness. PISTUEO means to trust in and rely upon, commit
to the charge of, confide in, have a mental persuasion. This is HUGE!!! You
must believe with your heart that the person you are ministering to is the
person God created them to be. If you don't believe with your heart, your
attempts at helping the person will be void of the necessary power
required. Your attempt will be "HALF HEARTED". Hebrews 3:12-14 will
shed light on this. "So search your hearts every day, my brothers and
sisters, and make sure that none of you has evil or unbelief hiding within
you. For it will lead you astray, and make you unresponsive to the living
God. ¹³ This is the time to encourage each other to never be stubborn or
hardened by sin's deceitfulness. ¹⁴For we are mingled with the Messiah, if
we will continue unshaken in this confident assurance from the beginning
until the end" (TPT). I love this Scripture. "Evil" and "unbelief" both
cause us to become "unresponsive" to God. If you don't have The Spirit of

Truth supporting you in your efforts to defeat unwanted spirits, it's not going to bear any fruit. It's a heart issue. Remember that the addict is dealing with a sick heart (Proverbs 13:12). You literally need to have a "heart to heart" conversation and interaction. Your believing, healthy heart to their sick heart. If you were in the doctor's office because you were sick and the doctor walked in to examine you as sick as you were, how would you feel? **If your heart is not healthy enough to treat a sick heart, then start treating your own heart.**

HOPE

"For now we see but a faint reflection of riddles and
mysteries as though reflected in a mirror, but one day we will
see face-to-face. My understanding is incomplete now, but
one day I will understand everything, just as everything about
me has been fully understood. ¹³ Until then, there are three
*things that remain: faith, **hope**, and love—yet love surpasses*
them all. So above all else, let love be the beautiful prize for
which you run."
— 1 Corinthians 13:12-13, TPT

HERE'S WHERE THE RUBBER MEETS the road. How do you restore hope in a hopeless person? Of course it's different for everyone, but there are some fundamentals that can be the foundation of this rather daunting task. First we need to understand what hope really is. Hope is eager anticipation of something good. According to Baker's Evangelical Biblical Dictionary, hope means, "To trust in, wait for, look for, or desire something or someone; or to expect something beneficial in the future." Hope is often seen as a wish. A wish is wanting something that you don't believe you'll receive. Hope is not a wish. Hope requires heart deep belief, or faith if you prefer. To me belief and faith are interchangeable words. We wish upon a star, but we put our hope in the Lord.

This may sound selfish or crazy at first, but it's NOT in any way. IT STARTS WITH YOU. As stated earlier in this book, we must NOT confirm, reinforce, or support the lies that unwanted spirits tell. We must NOT let life's circumstances or the world's view shape our opinions or sight of the hopeless person in our lives. Let's look at how to equip ourselves with the capacity to see the hopeless the way God sees them. Holy Spirit can work in every person as He sees fit. These are two ways that have been revealed to me. Which comes first will be up to you and Him. Both of these methods work for me, depending on my internal/spiritual condition.

The first way I'll discuss can sometimes work best while we're practicing the second way. Believe the Bible. Genesis 1:26-28 and Genesis 2:7 will be my point of reference. God created ALL of us in His image and likeness. This is where we need to look at ourselves. Do we understand God's nature, personality, character, and attributes? If we are to understand ourselves and other people, we need to seek knowledge of Him. To know Him is to know ourselves and others. That is, if we believe we are created in His image and likeness. This requires a considerable amount of undoing. Most of us have been taught to be sin conscious instead of love/God conscious. This means that we believe God sees our sin and can't love us as a result of our sin. This is NOT the truth. It's yet another lie. This may help: "Then the Lord God formed man of dust from the ground, and breathed into his nostrils the breath of life; and man became a living being" (Genesis 2:7, NASB). In the creation story (Genesis 1-3), God spoke everything into existence, except us. God "formed man" and "breathed into his nostrils the breath of life."

God created us very intimately. We're the only part of His massive creation that He touched, or formed, and breathed life into. It doesn't say that He did this to some of us, He created us ALL this way. In order to give hope to the hopeless, we first must see them as God created them to be. We must speak to that person. Instead of saying, "you look terrible," say "you are created wonderfully." Instead of saying "you need to stop..." say "His plan for your life is brilliant." Instead of saying, "you're killing yourself," say "I love you." Use words associated with God. Words like love, forgiveness, grace, mercy, compassion, passion, faith, hope, strength, glory (glorious), and did I mention LOVE.

Think of the fruit that can come from saying, "I forgive you," instead of saying "you're hurting/killing me." To say to your loved one, "you are so compassionate" isn't lying. Not living in God's image and likeness is the lie. Some other key statements may sound like this: "you're so strong," "you have so much faith," "hope lives inside of you," "love pours out of your heart." Seeking the Kingdom of Heaven will enable us to know God's character. In turn we will know everyone's character. This may sound like a stretch, considering some of the evil in the world, but we know His ways are MUCH different and better than our ways.

I know that when I was imprisoned, I needed ALL the forgiveness, grace, mercy, and love I could get. I can't say that I deserved grace, mercy, forgiveness, and love more than anyone else that has ever sinned. Tough to wrap our minds around this, so try to wrap your heart around this idea. Don't forget, the goal is to instill hope, so that the addict can grab a hold of it and allow God to pull them out of the costume of lies and false identity that they are trapped in.

The second way of seeing how God sees the hopeless is to ask Him to show you how He sees them. This is the part that is going to sound selfish, because it doesn't have much to do with anyone else, but you. Practice on yourself first. It's perhaps the scariest prayer we could ever pray. The first time I prayed for God to show me how He sees me, I was sin conscious. I saw all my sin and it was horrific. I saw God through the sin conscious, religious lens that He was introduced to me through. I saw Him as a cosmic policeman in the sky waiting to clobber me with His club every time I sinned. Then He started to "undo" me. Holy Spirit started to break off the old covenant, law based, self-help program, behave yourself into Heaven, religious teaching that I had received in church as a child. He taught me, and continues to teach me, who I am in Him and who He is in me. He taught me to be conscious of God's love for me instead of my sin.

After a while, I felt led to ask Him again to show me how He sees me. I reluctantly did so. This time I saw a glimpse of how He saw me and it was the most beautiful thing I've ever seen. He only shows me glimpses, because my human capacity can't handle or hold His truth about me. I felt His embrace and His love for me. These times with Him are VERY emotional and intimate. I usually need time to recover. Shame, guilt, abandonment, and everything and anything that bound me on earth fell off and landed on the ground around me like chains. This happened about 4 years into my freedom. I continue to pray this prayer often.

I also pray for Him to show me how He sees other people. Sometimes He shows me. When He does, I can speak into that person's identity and destiny. This is new covenant prophecy. Old covenant prophecy foretold of

Jesus, new covenant prophecy edifies, encourages, and helps people align themselves with God's plan for them. I can love them in a way I never thought possible.

Understanding who you are in Him and who He is in you, makes it possible to minister to others in a way that is beyond our mind's comprehension. Keep your mind out of it. Your heart will understand completely. This happens because, Holy Spirit is intertwined with our spirit. By positioning yourself in Him, and knowing He's in you, you are equipped to minister in ways you never thought possible.

It's a lie that taking care of yourself is selfish. If you are functioning at 75% of your capacity, then you're cheating everyone of 25% of you. Our loved ones deserve 100% of our capacity. Don't get hung up on the lie that taking care of yourself physically, emotionally, and most of all spiritually is selfish. The people you minister to need 100% of you. Being able to see how God sees you, knowing His thoughts of you, and being in close, intimate, fellowship with Him will certainly have you running at 100% capacity.

Hopelessness is yeast of hell. It spreads throughout the entire creation... if we let it. We cannot bring hope to the hopeless without hope in us. "Living within you is the Christ who floods you with the expectation of glory! This mystery of Christ, embedded within us, becomes a heavenly treasure chest of hope filled with the riches of glory for his people, and God wants everyone to know it!" (Colossians 1:27, TPT) If we can't connect to God or believe the Bible we can't offer any help to the hopeless. Our ministry or our attempts at helping will be rooted in the world's view and that is steeped in lies. Pointing out how hopeless, worthless, hurtful, unlikable, and terrible the addict is doesn't combat their hopelessness. Hope combats their hopelessness. Our hope is in the Lord, so get in the Lord. Let Him flow through you.

LOVE

"For now we see but a faint reflection of riddles and
mysteries as though reflected in a mirror, but one day we will
see face-to-face. My understanding is incomplete now, but
one day I will understand everything, just as everything about
me has been fully understood. ¹³ *Until then, there are three*
*things that remain: faith, hope, and **love**—yet **love** surpasses*
*them all. So above all else, let **love** be the beautiful prize for*
which you run."
— *1 Corinthians 13:12-13, TPT*

YOU NEED TO BELIEVE THAT GOD will use you in this way. To partner with Him, means that you must buy into His ways. God is love. His ultimate weapon is love. We mistake love for a feeling, when it is actually a choice. We choose to love based on the character and nature of the person, which is Christ like. We can't base our love on how the person makes us feel. That isn't fair to anyone. Praise God that His love for me isn't contingent upon what I do or how I make Him feel. Biblical love is holding someone's well-being in higher regard than your own. That's why we put our hope in God.

It bears repeating... God is love. "Agape," the love theme of the Bible, can only be defined by the nature of God. John affirms that "God is love" (1 John 4:8). God does not merely love; he is love. Everything that God does flows from His love. There's a reason why love is listed last in faith, hope, and love. Ultimately the love of God prevails. If you are able to receive the love God has for you, it will pour out of you and touch everyone that encounters you. It is love that equips us, sustains us, and empowers us. If we truly love the person we are ministering to, it will be easy to speak life into them. It will be easy to speak hope into them.

The majority of the Bible describes God's love, so I've opted out of quoting Scriptures. I will share that I know beyond a shadow of doubt that God loves me and I love Him. My heart knows Him, loves Him, and knows His love for me. It took a while for my heart to receive Him to this measure. I think we all know that God loves us in our minds, but life changed for me once my heart believed. I know that it was His love for me that delivered me and saved me. I know that His love sustains me and keeps me in His refuge. I've learned to love Him and people. More importantly, I've learned to ask Him to increase my desire to love Him and people. There's no better resource, when trying to love God and people, then Love itself.

PART THREE: THE POWER OF TESTIMONY

TESTIMONY

*"What I say to you in the dark, repeat in broad daylight, and
what you hear in a whisper, announce it publicly."*
— Matthew 10:27, TPT

START OFF SMALL. If you come on too strong, or different, your loved one will become suspicious. I experienced this with a relative of mine. They were a regular, excessive drinker. When I spoke to them I would ask things like "How's it going with drinking?" I would ask "Don't you think it's time to stop?" Again, this line of questioning does nothing but offend the captive. It's like going into the prison system and asking the inmates, "Why don't you just leave?" Remember that they can't. They know they need too, but they can't, because they are hopeless. One day while praying, I was quiet just long enough to give Him a word in edgewise and I heard "Just love them." WHAT???!!! Just love them. It didn't even register until days later. Finally, I called my relative and said, "I was just calling to tell you that I love you and that I was thinking about you." After awkward silence, I said "Ok, talk to you later" and hung up. Each time I did this, which wasn't often at first, the awkward silence decreased and my relative started to welcome the affectionate words of encouragement. Our conversations started to become more meaningful and void of offense. Our conversations were enjoyable, pleasant, and loving. This started in November. The following April, 5 months later, I was out of town at a spiritual conference and I had a vision of this relative being freed from captivity. In the vision I saw how much God loved them. It was very emotional, so I called them and told them of the vision. During this very emotional phone call, my relative told me that they and their spouse had stopped drinking just a week or so before this phone call. They explained that "It just left them." That "They were done with drinking." At that point significant praise to God rang out. Of course this is God's doing, but my relative did say that my phone calls of loving encouragement changed the landscape of their "normal life." It's all about hope, loving, and speaking to the person God created that person to be. My relative and their spouse are still enjoying their freedom today, several years later.

My wife and I have experienced this in many different situations and circumstances. We once had a couple to our home for dinner that had been struggling. To make a long story short, the wife of the couple called my wife the next day and asked, "What did you do to my husband?" She claimed that he had returned to the loving, God-loving husband that he was prior to the problems. Actually, even better. My wife and I had initially disregarded the report we received from the wife that initiated the dinner. They were both believing lies, so we opted out of listening to the report that we saw was shrouded in lies and world view. We prayed and asked for Holy Ghost to show us who the husband was to Him and for us to speak to that identity. There was no vision or words or light show. They came over, we spoke to the person that we saw walk into our home and it just so happened that it was the person that the husband was intended to be. Just like that, he was freed from the costume of lies that he was believing about himself. I'm sharing these testimonies with you, because testimony gives God a chance to repeat His miracles. That's right folks, these are miracles. Salvation isn't a one and done gift. Jesus offers us salvations.

One more testimony. A friend's son was in over his head in addiction. She had a vision of her son that he was a preacher. She believed her vision, she believed prophecy is still for now, and she believed God. She started talking to him as though he was already a preacher. She would refer to him as "My little preacher." She spoke directly to the person that God showed her he was. The whole time he was imprisoned by unwanted spirits. It didn't take long. Her son was freed and he became a preacher. These testimonies are to help you understand your roll and partnership with Holy Spirit. Holy Spirit is the power behind the salvation and freedom, but you are the instrument in which the power flows through.

CONCLUSION

WHAT A THRILL IT IS TO SEE someone freed from the captivity of addiction. Especially if it's a loved one. For years I've watched good hearted people support the very lies that keep addicts imprisoned. It's very hard to relate to or understand the addicted. The more you understand about the inter-workings of the addict, the better you can serve them. God turns all things to good. In the process of helping others, you will receive the supernatural council of Holy Spirit. You too will receive breakthrough and a touch from God. There is so much to be learned about the Kingdom and His ways. Opening our hearts to Him and allowing Him to shape, mold, and hold our hearts will not only help you, but everyone around you.

Loving people is difficult to do in this religious culture of judgement and acceptance of sin. It's important to keep ourselves in good spiritual condition. Recalibrating our hearts and minds so that what matters to Him, matters to us. Helping those in need by sharing God's love with them. Not preaching at the person, or trying to "snap them out of it", but literally sharing the love that we've received from Him. To position ourselves in such a way that we can be conduits of all that He is. The second greatest commandment is to "love your neighbor as yourself" (Matthew 22:39). This means that we must love ourselves in order to love others. There's only one way for that to happen... Jesus. Another version of the second greatest commandment reads, "Love each other just as much as I have loved you." (John 13:34 TPT) The solution to loving others well is to allow Jesus to love us. The idea that my heart/spirit needs to be in union with Him. As I enter into deeper union with Him, I can love and help others the way He loves and helps me.

My personal goal is to love and help others as much and in the same way Jesus loves and helps me. I'm banking on Him to have forgiveness, grace, mercy, patience, compassion, and most of all love for me when it comes to my eternal life. As I receive these gifts from Him, I can extend them to others. His ways are better than our ways. The addict in your life isn't in their right identity or custom. They are believing lies that keep them imprisoned. Set them free by "pulling them out of it". May God bless you in this process of redemption and reconciliation.

Made in the USA
Middletown, DE
21 August 2023

37096808R00024